YOUNG CHILDREN RAP

To Learn About
Famous African-Americans

by Chris Meissel

Incentive Publications, Inc.
Nashville, Tennessee

Cover and illustrations by Susan Eaddy
Edited by Cherrie Farnette and Jan Keeling

Library of Congress Catalog Card Number: 92-74231
ISBN 0-86530-265-0

Table of Contents

PREFACE

The rhymes and activities in *Famous African-Americans* were developed in response to a perceived lack of resources for teaching young children about notable African-Americans. Young children learn best through rhyme, repetition, and movement, and the rhymes and activities in this book can be used effectively with preschool-age children and those in the early primary grades.

Each famous African-American selection includes a brief biographical statement about the individual, a learning rhyme, comprehension questions, and thematic activities associated with the individual's accomplishments. Science, math, and gross motor activities are provided for basic skill development, while enrichment exercises encourage connections with music, drama, and art. Thematic extension activities provide suggestions for field trips, guest speakers, food-related activities, and circle time. These activities can be used, modified, and expanded to meet the needs of the class.

The learning rhymes are raps! Young children will delight in a lively beat and energetic rhythms while they learn about good role models and develop self-esteem. It is important to know how to present these raps—it is most important to keep a strong regular beat, usually four heavy beats to a line. You will find the syllables for these down-beats in italics. You may wish to clap to the beat or provide the children with simple percussion instruments. Don't be alarmed if the unaccented syllables seem somewhat irregular. Just "let them fall where they may," saying them quickly if there are a *lot* of them between beats—as long as you emphasize the four major beats and keep them regular, you'll be fine. You will enjoy seeing the fun your children have with these learning raps.

This book, of course, includes only some of the many famous African-Americans who have made significant contributions to their country. You will be able to devise ways to present other African-Americans whose lives should be shared with young children. As are our children, teachers are creative, exciting, and intuitive people!

Henry "Hank" Aaron

Henry Louis Aaron was born in Mobile, Alabama, in 1934. He secured a place in the Baseball Hall of Fame by leading the National League in home runs four different seasons, winning the league batting championship twice, and holding, in 1974, the major league career record for runs batted in at 2,297. While playing for the Braves and the Milwaukee Brewers, he set the record for home runs made in one season by hitting 715 home runs.

Henry "Hank" Aaron was the "Home Run King."

He stepped to the plate with a homerun swing.

When he stepped to the plate, you could see that he was great,

And he ran around the bases as the ball took wing.

Reading

Read this poem to the students. Now read the poem **again**, this time letting the students provide the rhyming words "King," "swing," "great," and "wing."

Rhyme

1. Which word rhymes with king? (swing)
2. Which word rhymes with plate? (great)
3. Which word rhymes with air? (fair)

Comprehension

1. What is the name of this person? (Henry "Hank" Aaron)
2. What did Henry Aaron do? (played baseball)
3. What did Henry Aaron do to the baseball? (any answer)
4. Why do you think people loved to see him play? (any answer)

Music

Have the students sing "Take Me Out To The Ball Game."

Gross Motor

Obtain a plastic ball and bat. Let the students take turns throwing, catching, and hitting the ball. Soft sponge balls can be used inside the classroom.

Science

Obtain an old baseball and a razor blade to take apart the ball. Gather the students in a group and show them what is inside a baseball.

Field Trip

If you are fortunate enough to live near the headquarters of a Farm or Minor League (or high school) baseball team, take your students to watch the team practice. Videotapes about baseball can be rented and viewed in the classroom if an actual team is not available for class observation. Discuss what the players in the various playing positions do during a game.

Game

Obtain a baseball and three solid containers. Gather the students in a circle. Put the baseball in one of the containers. Scramble the containers and pick one student to guess which container hides the baseball.

Kareem Abdul-Jabbar

Kareem Abdul-Jabbar (Ferdinand Lewis Alcindor, Jr.), born in New York City in 1947, is one of the greatest centers in basketball history. Standing 7 feet, 2 inches tall, he played in the National Basketball Association from 1969–1989. During this time he scored a record 38,387 points, was twice the leader in NBA scoring, and was named the league's most valuable player six times.

Kareem Abdul-Jabbar *stood* very *tall.*

Kareem Abdul-Jabbar *played* basket*ball.*

Kareem Abdul-Jabbar *shot* from a*far.*

He was a *fa*mous *basket*ball *star!*

Reading

Read the poem to the students. Then read the poem a second time, letting the students insert the rhyming words "fall" and "star."

Rhyme

1. Which word rhymes with tall? (basketball)
2. Which word rhymes with afar? (star)
3. Can you think of any other words that rhyme with or sound the same as basketball or tall?
4. Can you think of any other words that rhyme with or sound the same as afar or star?

Comprehension

1. What is the name of this person? (Kareem Abdul-Jabbar)

2. What did Kareem Abdul-Jabbar do? (played basketball)
3. Do you think he is a tall man? (any answer) Why?
4. What did he shoot into the net? (a basketball)

Gross Motor

If possible, find a child-size basketball rim and take the students outside to practice "shooting" the ball into it. Practice "shots" can be made in the classroom by using a soft ball and a large round trash can.

Math

Have the students gather in a circle. Compare the heights of pairs of students. Have the students estimate who of each pair is taller. Then have the class members line up from tallest to shortest. Tape a large piece of paper to a door. Mark the students' heights on the paper. (Make sure names and date are written next to the marks.)

Circle

Show portions of a videotaped baseball game to the class. Compare the students' observations.

Art

Let the students make "basketballs." Cut out a round white circle for each student. Provide paints and crayons of different colors. Allow the students to decide how they want to decorate their basketballs. Combine red and yellow paint to make the orange "basketball color."

Muhammad Ali

Muhammad Ali was born Cassius M. Clay in 1942 in Louisville, Kentucky. Ali was a famous American heavyweight boxer who became the first to win the world heavyweight championship four times. A colorful and controversial champion, Ali bragged about his ability and made up poems about his opponents.

There *once* was a *man* named Mu*ham*mad Al*i*.

He could "*float* like a *butterfly*" and "*sting* like a *bee*."

Be*fore* he changed his *name,* he was *called* Cassius Clay.

He *won* a gold *med*al for the *U.S.A.!*

Rhyme
1. Which word rhymes with Ali? (bee)
2. Which word rhymes with Clay? (U.S.A.)
3. What other words rhyme with Clay? (play, say, etc.)
4. What other words rhyme with Ali? (see, tree, me, etc.)

Comprehension
1. What is the name of this person? (Muhammad Ali)
2. What did he do? (fight, box)
3. What could he "float" like? (a butterfly)
4. What could he "sting" like? (a bee)
5. How many gold medals did he win? (one)

Drama

Have students pretend they are butterflies. Let them move freely around the classroom. Then have them pretend they are bees as they move around the classroom.

Science & Language

If possible, obtain a butterfly and a bee and place them in separate jars. If real insects are not available, use photographs, drawings, or puppets. Ask the group to describe each insect: how it moves, the sounds it makes, where it lives, and what it does. Create a group language experience story.

Play Extension

Have the students pretend they are getting their hands wrapped like boxers. Obtain several large rolls of gauze and medical tape. (Bathroom tissue and masking tape can be used.) Wrap one of each student's hands. Discuss why this is done by boxers before fighting.

Art

Have your students make American flags. Show them a model of the flag. Pass out white, red, and blue paper, and help the children cut out rectangle stripes and stars. Provide paste and help them assemble their flags.

Circle

Practice reciting the "Pledge of Allegiance." Explain to the students why we pledge our allegiance to the U.S. flag.

Marian Anderson

Marian Anderson was born in Philadelphia, Pennsylvania, in 1902. She was an American contralto and performed in concerts in Europe and throughout the United States. She was the first black American to sing a leading role at the Metropolitan Opera of New York City.

Marian Anderson sang like a bird.

People loved to hear her as she sang every word!

Though *born* in Phila*del*phia, she *traveled* near and *far.*

And she *sang* so beautiful*ly,* she be*came* a *star!*

Rhyme
1. Which word rhymes with bird? (word)
2. Which word rhymes with far? (star)
3. How many times do you see the word *star* here? (one)

Comprehension
1. What is the name of this person? (Marian Anderson)
2. What did she do? (sing)
3. Did she sing like a bird or a frog? (a bird)
4. Do you think people liked to hear her sing? (any answer)

Drama
Allow the students to perform in front of one another. Using a real or imaginary microphone, have students practice singing or act as though they are singing. Recordings of familiar songs

can be provided to encourage the shy singers. A radio can add fun to the drama by providing an unexpected song to "sing."

Art

Have students make their own microphones. Obtain styrofoam balls and wooden dowels. Cut the wooden dowels into 8-inch strips. Have the students paint their styrofoam balls and stick the dowels into the foam.

Science

Hook a microphone to a tape recorder. Have students say or sing something into the microphone, first in a loud voice and then softly. Play the recording back to the group. Ask the students to discuss the different sounds they hear. Other ways to vary vocal sound recordings are to have children:
- talk through a piece of cloth,
- record from behind a cabinet or curtain,
- talk with their backs to the microphone,
- mumble, or
- speak from a distance of four feet or more from the microphone.

Discuss why it is important for a performer to speak or sing clearly and directly into a microphone.

Extending Activity

Take the students to a local musical performance or let them watch a musical video in the classroom. Let the students see how different people sing. Compare their observations.

15

Louis Armstrong

Louis Armstrong (1898?-1971), also known as "Satchmo," was born in New Orleans, Louisiana. He was a famous American jazz musician who played the trumpet, led a band, and composed music. He popularized "scat" singing and made numerous hit records, including "Hello, Dolly" and "Mack the Knife."

Louis Armstrong, I'm your fan.

Play that trumpet as loud as you can.

Louis, we love your smile and big cheeks.

We could listen to your music every day and every week!

Reading

Total group or divided coral repetition should be given each two-line segment (each sentence) of the poem.

Rhyme

1. Which word rhymes with fan? (can)
2. Which word rhymes with cheeks? (week)
3. What other words rhyme with fan? (man, pan, etc.)
4. What other words rhyme with week? (seek, sneak, etc.)

Comprehension

1. What is the name of this person? (Louis Armstrong)
2. What did he do? (play the trumpet)
3. Did he have big cheeks? (yes)

Music

If possible, bring a trumpet to class. Let the students touch it and describe it. Blow into it to show the students how it works. Observe their reactions. Explain how your cheeks can get big when you are about to blow into it.

For an exciting musical and learning event, invite an upper-grade student to perform for the group. The group can also listen to and discuss recordings of trumpet and jazz instrumentals.

Science

Pass out lengths of cardboard tubing from paper product rolls and discuss with students how the air moves when they blow straight through the tubing. Then have them "buzz" their lips as they blow through the tubing, as a trumpet-player does when blowing into a trumpet. Ask them to describe what they think the air does when they do this.

Math

Blow up a balloon and tie it. Gather the students in a circle. Tell the students that you are going to throw the balloon high into the air. When you throw the balloon, see how high you can count before it lands on the ground.

Gross Motor

Encourage students to dance while listening to trumpet and jazz music. This interpretive dancing can be done with or without partners.

Arthur Ashe

Arthur Ashe was born in 1943 in Richmond, Virginia. He became a tennis player and was the first black man to win the U.S. men's national singles championship (in 1968) and the Wimbledon singles championship (in 1975). He wrote a three-volume history of American black athletes called *A Hard Road To Glory*.

Arthur, Arthur, Ashe, Ashe, Ashe!

Hit the tennis ball with a smash, smash, smash!

Arthur, Arthur, win, win, win!

Hit your serve with a spin, spin, spin!

Arthur, Arthur, wow, wow, wow!

Listen to the crowd and bow, bow, bow!

Reading

Read the poem to the group. Divide the group into 3 choral sections. Each section will join in on one of the following three groups of words as you read the poem a second time.

- "Ashe, Ashe, Ashe" and "smash, smash, smash"
- "win, win, win" and "spin, spin, spin"
- "wow, wow, wow" and "bow, bow, bow"

Rhyme

Ask, "Which word rhymes with Ashe?" (smash) "Win?" (spin) "Wow?" (bow)

Comprehension

1. What is the name of this person? (Arthur Ashe)
2. What game did Arthur Ashe play? (tennis)
3. What did he do with the ball? (smashed it)

4. What did Arthur Ashe do before the crowd? (he bowed)
5. How did he hit his serve? (with a spin)

Science

Bring a tennis racket and some tennis balls to the class. Pass these around and ask the students to describe them. Ask:

"What do you think the strings are used for?"

"Why does this ball come back when you drop it?"

"Is this tennis ball hard or soft?"

"Why is this ball yellow and fluffy?"

It is important to allow the students to give you a variety of responses. Any response is a good response.

Math

Estimation: Put several tennis balls in a big jar. Have the students estimate the number. Make a graph using the students' responses.

Gross Motor

Collect a bag of tennis balls and take the students outside to a basketball court or an area with a cement surface. Give a tennis ball to each student. The students can practice bouncing, throwing, and catching the tennis balls.

Extended Activity

Take the students to a nearby tennis court and have them watch people playing tennis. Record their observations. If you do not have any courts nearby, tape a tennis match on television or obtain a tennis video and let the students watch it at school.

Benjamin Banneker

Benjamin Banneker (1731-1806) was born near Baltimore, Maryland. He became an accomplished mathematician, astronomer, farmer, and surveyor, and carved from wood a remarkable clock that kept perfect time for fifty years. Banneker helped survey the site of the District of Columbia and published an almanac which was praised by Thomas Jefferson. He defended the intellectual equality of black people.

Hickory, dickory, dock,

Banneker made a good clock.

Benjamin Banneker loved

Math and the stars above.

Hickory, dickory, dart,

Banneker was very smart.

Reading

Initial reading of the poem should be done before the entire group. On second reading, each two-line segment can be echoed by the group. For the third reading, the second line of each segment should be supplied by the student choral group.

Rhyme

Ask the students which word rhymes with dock (clock), loved (above), and dart (smart).

Comprehension

1. What is the name of this person? (Benjamin Banneker)
2. What did Benjamin Banneker make? (a good clock)
3. What did Benjamin Banneker love? (the stars, or math)
4. What is math? (numbers)
5. What is a clock used for? (to tell time)

Art

Cut out big white circles for all the students. Pass out crayons and have the students make their own clocks. Fold the circles in half and then in half again to create lines for placing the numbers 3, 6, 9, and 12 on the unfolded clock.

Science

Collect as many 2-liter plastic bottles as possible. Fill one 2-liter bottle halfway up with sand. Fasten this bottle to an empty 2-liter bottle, using glue, adhesive tape, or a plastic cap designed to hold them together. Make several of these "sand timers." Have the students estimate how long it will take for one bottle to empty and the other to fill.

Math

Obtain a large clock without the glass cover. Have the students practice moving the long hand to a number you call out. For example, if you say "2," the student should move the long hand to the number 2.

Circle

Have students join hands to form a circle. Bring a timer to the circle and set it to go off after one minute passes. Have the students walk around the circle for one minute until the timer goes off. Set the timer for two minutes and have the students lie down and close their eyes for two minutes until the timer goes off. You may want to make up your own activities with time limits.

Mary McLeod Bethune

Mary McLeod Bethune (1875-1955) was born in Mayesville, South Carolina. She became an educator who taught in Georgia and Florida and co-founded Bethune-Cookman College. She was director of the Division of Negro Affairs of the National Youth Administration and fought for the desegregation of schools.

Mary Bethune worked *all* her *life.*

She *saw* some *good* times, she *saw* some *strife.*

She be*lieved* in edu*cation* for the *peo*ple of the *nation,*

And she *helped* them find *knowl*edge by *founding* a *col*lege.

Rhyme
1. Which word rhymes with life? (strife)
2. Which word rhymes with college? (knowledge)
3. Which word rhymes with education? (nation)

Comprehension
1. What is the name of this person? (Mary McLeod Bethune)
2. What did she do? (any acceptable answer)
3. What was the name of the college she founded? (Bethune-Cookman College)
4. Why did she establish this college? (for people to find knowledge, or to provide education for black people)

Drama
Gather the students in a circle. Encourage students to take

turns being the "teacher" and leading circle exercises (fingerplay, calendar, poem, nursery rhyme, or song).

Art

Pass out construction paper, glue, crayons, and coffee stirrers. Have the students construct a model of a college campus.

Field Trip

If possible, take the students to a local college or university. Explain that this is a place where they can prepare for a career. Let the students see the library and tour the campus. If a college trip is not possible, take a tour of your own school "campus." Divide into groups to discuss different types of learning that take place in different parts of the school.

Math

Have the students count how many buildings they see on campus. If you tour your own school campus, count the rooms.

Circle

Ask students to share what they observed on the field trip. Do a language experience story (for group reading and illustrating). Ask the students what they want to be when they grow up and discuss what types of education they will need.

23

Guion Bluford

Guion S. Bluford was born in Philadelphia, Pennsylvania, in 1942. As a member of the U.S. Air Force, Bluford flew 144 missions in the Vietnam War. He later joined the National Aeronautics Space Administration (NASA) and became the first black American crew member of a U.S. space shuttle. This shuttle, called "Challenger," was launched in 1983.

Guion Bluford loved to fly, fly, fly!

He *flew* in an *airplane* in the *sky*, sky, *sky!*

He *flew* in a *space*ship out of *sight*, sight, *sight*,

And re*turned* six days *later* in the *night*, night, *night!*

Rhyme
1. Which word rhymes with fly? (sky)
2. Which word rhymes with sight? (night)
3. Which other words rhyme with sight? (bite, light, etc.)

Comprehension
1. What is the name of this person? (Guion Bluford)
2. What did he fly? (an airplane or spaceship)
3. Does a spaceship fly high or low? (high)
4. How many days did it take Guion Bluford to return in the night? (six)

Circle
Divide into groups to discuss the adventure of flying. Look for and list description words that can be used for such experiences. Talk about the adventure of exploring and invite students to share about times and places that they have explored.

Art

Have the students make spaceships. Give each student a paper-product tube, pre-cut fins (construction paper), paint, and glue. Allow time for the students to paint their tubes. When the paint dries, help them glue their fins to the bottoms of the tubes.

Science

If possible, obtain a wooden airplane kit with rubber band propulsion. Let the students guess where it will go and how long it will stay in the air. If this type airplane is not available, any "flyable" airplane will do. (Paper airplanes will work quite well, they just won't travel as far.)

Math

Have your students work in groups to make airplanes out of small interlocking plastic blocks. Ask them to count the number of blocks in their airplanes.

Field Trip Possibilities

Field Trip 1: Take the students to an air and space museum. Let them observe different forms of flight. Invite them to share their observations.

Field Trip 2: Take the students to a local planetarium. Here the students can experience the stars!

Field Trip 3: Take the students to a local airport or airfield to observe the takeoffs and landings of airplanes. Discuss the sights and sounds of the airport.

Gwendolyn Brooks

Gwendolyn Brooks was born in Topeka, Kansas, in 1917. She grew up in Chicago. Brooks became a famous American poet and won the 1950 Pulitzer Prize for her poem *Annie Allen.*

Gwendolyn Brooks loved to write
During the day and into the night.
Her poetry won a Pulitzer Prize.
It brought tears to the judges' eyes.

Rhyme
1. Which word rhymes with write? (night)
2. Which word rhymes with prize? (eyes)
3. What other words rhyme with prize? (size, wise, etc.)

Comprehension
1. What is the name of this person? (Gwendolyn Brooks)
2. What did she do? (she wrote poetry)
3. What did she win? (a prize)
4. Was her writing beautiful? (yes)

Circle
Tell the students that Gwendolyn Brooks wrote about beautiful things. As a group discuss beautiful things and list examples on the board or on a chart tablet. Create sentences about the beautiful things discussed. Use rhyming words whenever possible.

Science

Collect magazines, newspapers, books, cards, coupons, labels, boxes, and letters. Give each student a sample of each. Lead a discussion about the different types of printed materials. Have the students describe different styles of writing and classify these into groups. (Examples: stories, advertisements, news articles, etc.)

Art

Give each student pens, markers, pencils, chalk, and crayons. Pass out yellow construction paper. Have the students practice writing samples of the different types of writing described and classified in the Science activity. Invite the students to share their creations.

Math

Gwendolyn Brooks wrote poetry books. Help the students make math books. Give each student five pieces of white 8½" x 11" paper and fifteen round cereal pieces. Instruct them to glue one cereal piece on one page, two pieces on the second page, and so on until the student reaches the fifth and final page. Write the word for the number of pieces at the bottom of each page. (The number of math book pages and cereal pieces and the complexity of this problem should be adjusted to the level of student competency.)

Field Trip

Take a walk around the schoolyard to collect leaves in a bag. Bring the leaves back to the classroom. Create a language experience story called "The Leaf Story." Ask each student to say something nice about the leaves. Remind them that Gwendolyn Brooks wrote about beautiful things. Write the students' remarks on chart paper to save for future group reading.

George Washington Carver

George Washington Carver (1864-1943) was born a slave in the state of Missouri. He became an American botanist, known especially for his research in industrial uses of the peanut and sweet potato. Carver developed more than 300 products from peanuts! He taught at the Tuskegee Institute and also worked to improve race relations.

George *Washington Carver* had a *teaching plan.*

He was a *pea*nut, and a *soy*bean, and a *sweet* potato *man.*

He *stud*ied his *crops* in the *dark* and in the *light*

So that *everyone's life* would be *better* and *bright.*

Reading
Echo: Have the students repeat each line of the poem after you speak it.
Choral: Once the class has finished the poem, recite the entire poem together.

Rhyme
1. Which word rhymes with man? (plan) light? (bright)
2. What other words rhyme with light? (sight, tight, etc.) man? (can, pan, fan, etc.)

Comprehension
1. What is the name of this person? (George Washington Carver)
2. What foods did he work with? (peanuts, soybeans, and sweet potatoes)
3. Where does peanut butter come from? (peanuts)
4. What are some things Carver did with soybeans, sweet potatoes, and peanuts? (any answer)

Science

Bring to class several potatoes and enough peanuts in shells for everyone in the group. Peel and cut the potatoes. Pass them around for the students to feel, break open, and smell. Follow the same procedure with the peanuts. Extend the discussion to include possible uses for potatoes and peanuts. Ask students to share the ways they use these products in their own homes.

Math

Give each student plenty of soybeans or peanuts and a plastic cup. Practice counting with your students by calling out numbers and having each student place the correct number of beans in his or her plastic cup. Make up simple math problems using the beans.

Circle

Gather the students in a circle. Play "Hot Potato" (using a potato at room temperature) with the students. The student that drops it will sit out. The last student to remain in the circle is the winner.

Food

Choose some ways to prepare and eat potato and peanut foods. Examples:

- French fried potatoes
- Sweet potatoes with marshmallows
- Peanut butter and crackers
- Peanut butter on celery sticks
- Peanuts in green salads

Ray Charles

Ray Charles was born in Albany, Georgia, in 1930 as Ray Charles Robinson. Though he became blind at the age of seven, he grew up to be a famous American singer, songwriter, and pianist. Two of his best-known songs are "Georgia On My Mind" and "I Can't Stop Loving You."

There *is a man* who *cannot see.*

His *name's* Ray *Charles* to *you* and *me.*

He *plays* piano and *sings* a*loud*

And wher*ev*er he *goes* he *wows* the *crowd!*

Rhyme
1. Which word rhymes with see? (me)
2. Which word rhymes with loud? (crowd)
3. What other words rhyme with loud? (proud, cloud, etc.)

Comprehension
1. What is the name of this person? (Ray Charles)
2. What does Ray Charles do? (sings, plays the piano, writes songs)
3. How is Ray Charles different from some other musicians? (he is blind)

Circle

Discuss the difficulties of being blind. In what ways would blindness affect a person's life? How is someone who is blind the *same* as others who can see? (feelings, talents, etc.) Conclude the discussion by pointing out ways in which Ray Charles did not let his blindness interfere with his talent. Play some of Charles's music to illustrate this point and to add enjoyment to this circle time.

Math

If possible, bring a keyboard to class. Have class members count the keys, pressing them one by one as they count. Have them count the black keys and the white keys, then the groups of black keys.

Art

Have students draw or paint as you play music. Explain that there are different types of art forms (among them music, painting, drawing, singing), all of which can express feelings.

Field Trip

Ray Charles performed frequently on radio. Take your students to visit a radio station. Tell the students that the music in automobiles comes from radio stations.

Bill Cosby

Bill Cosby was born in Philadelphia, Pennsylvania, in 1937. He became a leading American entertainer, author, and TV producer. Some television shows in which he appeared include "I Spy," "The Cosby Show," and "Fat Albert." Books by Cosby include *Fatherhood*, *Time Flies*, and *Love and Marriage*. He is known and loved for his gentle humor about family life and childhood.

Bill *Cosby* is a *funny* man for *all* to *see!*

He *makes* me *laugh* when he's *on* TV!

His *show's* the *best*—it *can't* be *beat!*

Even in *reruns*, it's *still* a *treat!*

Rhyme
1. Which word rhymes with see? (TV)
2. Which word rhymes with beat? (treat)
3. What other words rhyme with beat? (meet, neat, etc.)

Comprehension
1. What is the name of this person? (Bill Cosby)
2. Where did people see him? (on stage or T.V.)
3. Did he make people laugh? (yes)

Circle Time
Tape an episode of the "Bill Cosby Show." Let the students watch it. Bill Cosby also created shows for public television which can be viewed in class.

Circle Time Game:

Bill Cosby's shows make people laugh. Play the "Laugh Game." Choose a student who will try to do something to make the class laugh. To make it a game, tell the class members to try very hard not to laugh.

Drama

Help the students make a "pretend television screen" by cutting a hole in a big cardboard box. Let the students take turns pretending they are on a T.V. show.

Art

Save plenty of shoeboxes. Cut out a square hole in the middle of each lid. Give each student some cellophane and tape and let the students make their own miniature televisions.

Benjamin Davis

Benjamin Davis (1877-1970) was born in Washington, D.C. He became a famous officer in the United States Army. He served as assistant to the inspector general of the army. He was the first black man to become a lieutenant general in the U.S. Armed Forces.

Benjamin *Davis wore* a gold *star*
On *each* of his *shoulders*. He *was* an *Army*
Man who *served* a *long* time a*go,*
And he *led* many *men* a*gainst* their *foe.*

Rhyme
1. Which word rhymes with ago? (foe)
2. What other words rhyme with ago? (blow, slow, etc.)

Comprehension
1. What is the name of this person? (Benjamin Davis)
2. What did he do? (any acceptable answer)
3. How many stars did Benjamin Davis have on each shoulder? (one)
4. What kind of man was he? (any answer)

Circle
Ask parents or visitors who are or have been in the military to talk to your students about military jobs. Encourage the students to ask questions.

Art

Teach the students to make "General's Stars." Cut out star shapes and give each student two. Direct students to paint their stars yellow. (Yellow construction paper can be used in place of paint.) When they are finished, tape one star to each of the students' shoulders.

Math

Obtain a collection of army or other miniature figures for this activity. (Many children can bring these from home.) Put these in a jar. Let the students estimate how many figures are in the jar. Make a graph of their guesses. Math problems can be modified by adding or taking away figures from the container.

Resource Person

Invite a spokesperson from the military or a National Guard unit to visit your classroom to tell about military life. Help the students develop a list of questions to ask the visitor.

Paul Lawrence Dunbar

Paul Lawrence Dunbar (1872-1906) was born in Dayton, Ohio. He was the son of an escaped Negro slave. Dunbar became a famous American poet and published many works on life in his time.

Paul *Dunbar used* his *pen* as a *tool*

To *write* poet*ry* all the *way* through *school.*

From *page* to *page* his *writing* was *witty,*

And you *might* even *say* each *word* was *pretty.*

Rhyme
1. Which word rhymes with tool? (school)
2. Which word rhymes with witty? (pretty)

Comprehension
1. What is the name of this person? (Paul Lawrence Dunbar)
2. What did he do? (he wrote poetry)
3. Why do you think people liked to read his books? (any answer)

Circle
Poetry often describes scenes, actions, or feelings depicted in works of art. Discuss the kinds of pictures that might be drawn to illustrate the following lines from a poem about Paul Lawrence Dunbar:

He used his pen as a tool.

His writing was witty.

Each word was pretty.

Draw pictures on the board for these poetry lines:

The fat cat sat on a hat.

The bug was snug in a rug.

Art

Teach the students to make their own books. Give each student about 5 sheets of 8½" x 11" white paper. Pass out paste, magazines, and scissors. Ask each student to make a certain kind of book. For example, some students may want to make an animal book, some a car book, and so forth. Let them cut and glue one picture per page. Have students write the word for that picture at the bottom of the page. When the activity is finished you may want to bind the books with staples or punch holes and tie them together with yarn or string.

Science

Bring in a variety of pens, pencils, crayons, markers, and chalk. Tell the students that these are all writing utensils. Have the students discuss the utensils' similarities and differences.

Drama

Gather the students in a group by the chalkboard. Play "Guess What I'm Drawing." Pick one student to go to the board and draw something. Let the class try to figure out what that student is drawing.

Resource Person

Invite a professional writer to your classroom to discuss writing as a career. Help students develop a list of questions to ask the visitor.

Duke Ellington

Edward Kennedy Ellington (1899-1974) was born in Washington, D.C. He was best known as "Duke" Ellington. He was a famous American band leader and jazz composer. Ellington wrote several motion picture scores and performed his music around the world.

R A P

One, two, three-four-five,

Ellington could *jive,* jive, *jive!*

He played *music* in a *band,* band, *band,*

Like *going* through *water* and *over land!*

Ellington's music would *ring,* ring, *ring,*

Every *time* you *heard* it you would *swing,* swing, *swing!*

One, two, three-four-five,

Duke's *music* is a*live!*

Reading

Read the poem to the students. On the second reading, ask the children to echo every other line. Divide the group in half, taking turns with each two-line segment.

Rhyme

1. Which words rhyme with five? (jive, alive)
2. Which word rhymes with band? (land)
3. Which word rhymes with ring? (swing)
4. What is another word that rhymes with five? (hive, etc.)

Comprehension

1. What is the name of this person? (Duke Ellington)

2. What did he do? (any answer dealing with music)
3. What musical instrument would you like to play? (any answer)

Music

Bring a trumpet, bongo drums, and, if possible, a keyboard to show the students the many instruments Duke Ellington could play. Let each student have a chance to play these instruments and to explore the ways that they differ.

Math

List on the chalkboard the numbers 1, 2, 3, 4, and 5. Ask:
1. What number comes before 2? (1)
2. What number comes after 4? (5)
3. What number comes before 3? (2)
4. What is the largest number listed? (5)

For advanced math students, make up more difficult problems using these numbers.

Science

Obtain a glass of water and a drum stick. Gather the students in a circle. Show the students that every time you hit the glass, ripples appear in the water. Tell them that sounds also make waves.

Food

Pass out bread sticks for snack time. Let the students pretend the bread sticks are drum sticks.

Patricia R. Harris

Patricia Roberts Harris (1924-1985) was born in Mattoon, Illinois. She became a lawyer and was the first black woman to hold a Cabinet post in the United States. Harris served as secretary of housing and urban development, and headed the Department of Health and Human Services. She was also the first black woman to serve as ambassador to a foreign country (Luxembourg).

R A P

Patricia *Harris* had a *wonderful voice.*

She was a *lawyer* and a *teacher* and a *leader* by *choice.*

Patricia *Harris,* we re*mem*ber who you *are,*

And we re*mem*ber if we *read,* we *will* go *far!*

Rhyme

1. Which word rhymes with voice? (choice)
2. Which word rhymes with are? (far)

Comprehension

1. What is the name of this person? (Patricia Harris)
2. What did she do? (she was a lawyer, teacher, and leader)
3. Did she have a good voice? (yes)
4. Why is it good to read? (any answer)

Circle

Discuss as a group what lawyers do. Include in the discussion what laws are, why we need them, and who makes them. Compare laws made for a community to those made for a classroom. List some classroom rules on the board and discuss why these rules are important. List some of the consequences of breaking these rules. Extend the discussion to include why there are lawyers to argue both sides of a case.

Drama

Pick one student to be the defendant and another to be the prosecutor. Hold up a piece of candy. Ask the defendant to tell you why he or she should eat the candy. Ask the prosecutor to tell you why the defendant shouldn't eat the candy. (Some possible arguments are that candy provides energy or that it is bad for the teeth.)

Field Trip

Take the class to visit a lawyer's office to interview a lawyer, or to a courtroom to observe courtroom procedures. Or you might invite a lawyer to the classroom to talk about what an attorney does.

Food

Bring supplies to decorate cookies, or ingredients to make various kinds of sandwiches. Let the students make their own creations. Then "judge" each student's work, awarding each one some kind of title (best-looking, most nutritious, most unusual, etc.).

41

Matthew A. Henson

Matthew Alexander Henson (1867-1955) was born in Maryland. He was the only American who accompanied Robert E. Peary on the final leg of his journey to the North Pole in 1909. Henson wrote a book about his twenty years of travel and experiences as Peary's companion on several expeditions. This book is entitled *A Negro Explorer at the North Pole.*

On a *very* cold *night* un*der* a *star,*

Matthew Henson traveled far.

Matthew Henson had a special goal:

He was a man who reached the North Pole.

Rhyme

1. Which word rhymes with star? (far)
2. Which word rhymes with goal? (Pole)
3. What other words rhyme with star? (car, bar, etc.)
4, What other words rhyme with Pole? (hole, coal, etc.)

Comprehension

1. What is the name of this person? (Matthew A. Henson)
2. Did he travel close by or far away? (far away)
3. Where did Matthew Henson travel? (North Pole)
4. What kind of place is the North Pole? (any answer)

Science

Allow students to experiment with ice cubes. First discuss the different properties of ice cubes—how they look, feel, taste, and smell. List descriptive words on the board or on a chart.

Use these words in sentences. Then break, crush, and melt ice. Talk about the changes that take place. Measure the time it takes for ice cubes to melt under different conditions (in the sun, in the shade, in water).

Art

Let the students try ice cube painting. Give each student an ice cube and colored fingerpaint. Let the students use the ice cubes to spread the paint on construction paper.

Field Trip

Take the students to a local restaurant or grocery store where they can go into a large freezer room. Let them discuss how it feels, and explain that this is something like the way it feels to be at the North Pole.

Drama

Take an imaginary trip to the North Pole. Provide pictures, filmstrips, and videos to show locations with ice and snow. Make a list of the articles you will need for the trip (warm clothes, tent, food, compass, etc.). As you begin your journey, encourage the students to make slow, climbing movements. Discuss what you might see on your journey.

Food

Let the students make snowcones. Provide crushed ice and one or more flavors of colored syrup. Fill cups with the crushed ice and pour the syrup over it. Enjoy!

Jesse Jackson

The Reverend Jesse Louis Jackson was born in 1941 in Greenville, South Carolina. He is a minister known for his efforts to promote equality and justice. Jackson became one of the foremost black political leaders in the United States. He ran for the U.S. presidency in 1983 and again in 1987.

Jesse Jackson can *preach, preach preach!*
He *travels* every*where* to *teach, teach, teach!*
He's a *man* with many *quotes, quotes, quotes!*
If you *listen* to *him,* take *notes, notes, notes!*

Rhyme
1. Which word rhymes with preach? (teach)
2. Which word rhymes with quotes? (notes)
3. What other words rhyme with quotes? (boats, floats, etc.)

Comprehension
1. What is the name of this person? (Jesse Jackson)
2. For what is he best known? (any acceptable answer)
3. What did Jesse Jackson want to change? (injustice)

Circle
Bring to class a videotape or tape recording of Jesse Jackson giving a speech. Let the students watch or listen. Point out Jackson's style of speaking and the response of the audience.

Art

Let the students make "Peace Doves." Cut out a dove shape for each student. Give the students cotton batting to glue in a thin layer on their doves. When they are finished, punch two holes on the top of each bird and thread with yarn to make a necklace.

Give each student round cereal pieces, beads, pretzels, and macaroni noodles. Pass out string and different colors of paints. Instruct the students to paint the materials and then to thread string through each piece to make a colorful African necklace.

Drama

Let the students listen to a recording of a Freedom March. Pick a student to play the part of Jesse Jackson. Ask everyone to pick a partner and to hold his or her hand. Let the children do a "Freedom March" around the school or theclassroom.

Food

Hold a "Jesse Jackson Peace Feast" in the classroom or outside. Provide crackers and peanut butter. Let each student pick another student to serve. Instruct each student to say something nice to the one she or he serves.

Mahalia Jackson

Mahalia Jackson (1911-1972) was born in New Orleans, Louisiana. She grew up to become one of the best-known gospel singers of the world. Jackson performed across the United States and internationally. She was also involved in the civil rights movement during the 1960's.

There *was* a gospel *sing*er who could *sing* very *loud.*

In *church* or in the *park,* she could *stir* the *crowd.*

Ma*halia Jack*son *was* her *name.*

Her *beautiful singing brought* her *fame.*

Rhyme
1. Which word rhymes with loud? (crowd)
2. Which word rhymes with name? (fame)
3. Can you think of other words to rhyme with loud or crowd?
4. Can you think of other words to rhyme with name or fame?

Comprehension
1. What is the name of this person? (Mahalia Jackson)
2. What did she do? (sing, participate in civil rights movement)
3. Where did Ms. Jackson sing? (in church or the park)
4. Do you think the crowd liked to listen to her sing? (any answer)

Music
Bring to class recordings of Mahalia Jackson. Let the

students listen to her. Discuss with the students her music and the response of her audience.

Science

Provide pictures of stained glass. Let the students compare stained-glass windows with the windows in the classroom. Discuss how windows are made and what might be the differences between making stained-glass windows and regular windows. Allow the students to design their own stained-glass windows using construction paper, cellophane, and tissue paper. This is a good activity to do in pairs or in small groups.

Art

Take the students outside and instruct them to collect small round stones. Pass out construction paper and paste. Ask the students to "build" their own churches.

Math

Tell the students to count the number of stones they used to construct their churches. Display the churches, and ask the students to estimate which church has the most stones and which has the fewest.

Field Trip

Take the students to a local church. Explain to them the meanings or functions of different materials and objects found in the church.

47

Frederick M. Jones

Frederick McKinley Jones was an American inventor. He invented an air-conditioning unit to be used for truck refrigeration in transporting perishable foods. This invention, patented in 1949, completely changed the food transport industry.

It *can* be *hot* in this *school, school, school!*

Frederick *Jones* knew *how* to keep *cool, cool, cool!*

The *air*-conditioner was *his* invention.

When you're *nice* and *cool,* Frederick *Jones* you can *mention!*

Rhyme
1. Which word rhymes with school? (cool)
2. Which word rhymes with invention? (mention)
3. What other words rhyme with school? (pool, tool, etc.)

Comprehension
1. What is the name of this person? (Frederick M. Jones)
2. What did he invent? (air conditioner for trucks)
3. What do air conditioners do? (cool the air)
4. Would you prefer to be in a cold place or a hot place? (any answer)

Circle
Discuss ways to keep things cool when the surrounding temperature is hot. Talk about what happens to plants and

animals when they get too hot. What happens to some foods and beverages ("perishables") when they get too hot? Ask the students to suggest different ways of keeping things cool. Discuss the importance of keeping certain things cool while transporting them from place to place.

Art

Let the students make fans. Give each student a piece of paper. Show them how to make folds. Encourage the students to decorate their fans by coloring them before making the folds.

Math

Ask the students to count the number of folds in the fans they made.

Science

Activity #1

Let the students make "air-conditioned rooms." Obtain shoeboxes and ice. Open the shoeboxes and line them with plastic (plastic bags can be used). Put the ice inside and replace the lids. Cut holes (large enough to fit a hand through) in the sides of the boxes. Let the students put their hands into the boxes through the holes. Discuss their findings.

Activity #2

Fill a glass with water and mark a line to show the water level. Let the glass of water sit for 10 minutes in front of a fan that is *not* turned on. Measure the change in the water level. Now fill the glass to the same line. Turn the fan on so that it blows over the surface of the glass for 10 minutes. Measure the difference in water level. Is it different this time? Discuss the results.

Scott Joplin

Scott Joplin (1868-1917) was a leading composer of ragtime music. He was born the son of a former slave in Texarkana, Texas. The score of the movie "The Sting" was based on his music. In 1976, Joplin was awarded a special Pulitzer citation for his contribution to American music.

Scott *Joplin* played *piano in* the *lights.*

With his *bold* piano-*playing,* he *reached* new *heights.*

He *played* and wrote *music* with a *special* kind of *"chime."*

We *know* him to*day* as "The *King* of Rag*time."*

Rhyme
1. Which word rhymes with lights? (heights)
2. Which word rhymes with chime? (Ragtime)
3. What other words rhyme with lights? (fights, kites, etc.)

Comprehension
1. What is the name of this person? (Scott Joplin)
2. What did Scott Joplin play? (piano)
3. Did Scott Joplin write music? (yes)
4. Do you think people liked his music? (any answer)

Gross Motor
As the students stand in a circle, play notes on a piano keyboard, or play a piano recording. Tell the students to jump high when they hear a high-sounding note. Have them stoop down low when they hear a low note.

Math

Take the students to see a piano in the school (if your school does not have a piano, use a keyboard). Let the students count the number of keys on the piano.

Science

Experiment with the varying sounds of a piano or keyboard. Let the students push the keys and discuss the difference in pitch, mood, volume, etc.

Art

Let the students make pianos. Pass out piano shapes pre-cut from black paper. Give each student white paint and a paintbrush. Let them paint the keys. (A picture of a keyboard will provide a helpful guide.)

Martin Luther King, Jr.

Martin Luther King, Jr. (1929-1968) was a famous black American Baptist minister. He was born in Atlanta, Georgia. King became the leader of the Civil Rights movement in the United States during the 1950's and was awarded the 1964 Nobel Prize for Peace for his efforts. King was assassinated in 1968. His birthday is observed as a national holiday.

Martin *Luther* King, *Junior* was a *very* great *man*.

He was *kind* and he was *caring* and he *always* had a *plan*.

He *did* a lot of *good* things for the *people* every *day*

And when he *saw* some *problems*, he would *never* run a*way*.

Rhyme
1. Which word rhymes with man? (plan)
2. Which word rhymes with day? (away)

Comprehension
1. What is the name of this person? (Martin Luther King, Jr.)
2. What kind of person was Dr. King? (kind, caring)
3. What kinds of things did he do for people? (any answer)
4. Did Dr. King run away from problems? (no)

Circle
Dr. King is famous for an important speech in which he repeated: "I have a dream." Ask the children to talk about their own dreams and their hopes for the future.

Art

Let the students make "freedom bracelets." Cut strips of 2" by 6" construction paper. Give each student some crayons and glue. When the students have finished coloring the strips they can glue them to form bracelets.

Food

Bring to class a loaf of bread that will break easily and evenly. Let each student break off a piece and give it to the person sitting next to him or her. When everyone has received a piece, discuss how it is good to share with others.

Music

Teach the students the song "We Shall Overcome."

Joe Louis

Joe Louis (1914-1981) was born Joe Louis Barrow in Lafayette, Alabama. He became a famous American boxer, and held the world heavyweight championship from 1937 to 1949. This was the longest reign ever in the history of boxing.

The *great* Joe *Louis* could *box, box, box!*

He could *knock* an op*ponent out* of his *socks!*

He *worked* very *hard* and he *stood* up *tall.*

Everyone he *fought* would *fall, fall, fall!*

Rhyme
1. Which word rhymes with box? (socks)
2. Which word rhymes with tall? (fall)
3. What other words rhyme with tall? (small, call, etc.)
4. What other words rhyme with box? (clocks, blocks, etc.)

Comprehension
1. What is the name of this person? (Joe Louis)
2. What did he do? (fight, box)
3. Do you think he hit very hard? (any answer)
4. Did he work hard? (yes) Why? (any answer)

Circle
Bring some boxing gloves to class. Let each student put one on and describe how it feels. Write the responses on chart paper.

Art

Let your students make their own boxing gloves. Give each student a small plastic bag (about the size of a lunch bag), some cotton batting, and a ribbon. Instruct them to stuff their bags with the cotton. Help them to put their hands in the "gloves," then tie them on with the ribbon.

Gross Motor

If possible, obtain a punching bag to hang in class. Let each student practice hitting the bag with the gloves. Tell them it is better to hit the bag than to take out one's frustration on another person or an animal.

Math

Count the number of times each student can hit the punching bag without missing. Make a graph.

Thurgood Marshall

Thurgood Marshall, born in Baltimore, Maryland, in 1908, was the first black American to serve as an Associate Justice on the United States Supreme Court (1967-1991). He presented the legal argument that resulted in the Supreme Court decision that racial segregation in public schools is unconstitutional.

Thurgood Marshall is a judge, judge, judge!
When it comes to the law, he doesn't budge!
He believes in doing what is right, right, right!
He helps the poor and weak to fight, fight, fight!

Rhyme
1. Which word rhymes with right? (fight)
2. Which word rhymes with judge? (budge)

Comprehension
1. What is the name of this person? (Thurgood Marshall)
2. What did he do? (he was a judge)
3. Ask the students what they think a judge does. (any answer)

Circle
Have the students gather in a circle. Discuss the importance of rules. Ask the students if they can name something that is good to do and something that is bad to do. Write down their observations on chart paper.

Art

Pass out modeling clay and sticks. Have each student make a gavel by pushing a stick into the clay. Tell the students that the judge uses the gavel to quiet everyone in the courtroom.

Field Trips

1. Take the students for a walk around the neighborhood streets. Emphasize the importance of safety. Ask students, "What would be the wrong thing to do?" (Possible answers: cross the street without looking both ways, fail to yield where there is a stop sign, etc.). "What would be the right things to do?" (Hold the hand of an adult, look both ways, etc.)

2. If it is possible, take the students to the local courthouse to show them a courtroom, the judge's chambers, and the jury box.

3. Visit a lawyer's office or that of a judge and ask questions about how the legal system works.

Jan Matzeliger

Jan Ernst Matzeliger (1852-1889) was a cobbler who lived in Philadelphia. He invented a machine that reduced the amount of time required to construct a pair of shoes. It shaped and fastened leather over the sole of a shoe.

Jan Matzeliger loved your *feet, feet, feet!*

He made *shoes* to wear in*doors* or on the *street, street, street!*

He was *known* to be *clev*er and *nice, nice, nice!*

Many *people* bought his *shoes* for a small *price, price, price!*

Rhyme
1. Which word rhymes with feet? (street)
2. Which word rhymes with nice? (price)
3. What other words rhyme with feet? (neat, beat, etc.)

Comprehension
1. What is the name of this person? (Jan Matzeliger)
2. What did he do? (made shoes)
3. What kind of shoes did he make? (any answer)
4. Did his shoes cost a lot? (no)

Gross Motor
Line the students up and have them take off their shoes. Roll a ball and let each student kick it. Have each student put his or her shoes back on and kick the ball again. Ask the

students to share how it feels to kick a ball with and without shoes. Discuss the functions of shoes (keep feet warm, protect from injury, etc.)

Art

Do "shoe painting." Have each student take off one shoe. Instruct students to trace around the shoe on construction paper and then to color the shape with crayons or paint. Let the students decorate the "top" of the shoe to match the shoes they are wearing.

Science 1

Let children make footprints in sand. The prints can be made with or without shoes. Fill the sunken prints with a mixture of plaster of paris. Initial the footprints so they can be identified as they dry. Remove from sand and compare prints. Line up in order of length and then by width.

Science 2

Find an old leather shoe. Using a razor blade, take it apart in front of the students. Point to each part of the shoe. Tell the students that Jan Matzeliger made a machine to glue the sole of the shoe to the other part.

Garrett Morgan

Garrett Augustus Morgan was born in Paris, Kentucky, in 1877. He invented the first traffic signal in 1923. It was purchased for $40,000 by the General Electric Corporation. Morgan also patented a breathing device in 1914 which was later used as a gas mask to protect firemen.

No one can *say* Garrett *Morgan* wasn't *bright.*

He in*vent*ed our *very* own *traffic light.*

When you *see* the red and *yellow* and the *green* glowing *bright,*

Think of the in*vent*or Garrett *Morgan,* day and *night!*

Reading

Echo: Say the first two lines and have the students repeat after you. Cup your hand to your ear to indicate when the students should repeat.

Choral: After you have gone through the entire poem, count to three and have students say the poem with you.

Rhyme

Ask the students which words rhyme with light. (bright, night) Name other words that rhyme with light. (kite, flight)

Comprehension

1. What is the name of this person? (Garrett Morgan)
2. What did Garrett Morgan invent? (a traffic light)
3. What do the colors on a traffic signal mean? (red: stop, yellow: slow down, green: go)

Art

Make a traffic light:

- Cut out three colored circles for each student: red, yellow, and green circles to indicate stop, slow down, and go.
- Pass out construction paper and paste.
- Instruct the students to make their traffic lights by pasting the colored circles to the construction paper.

In Motion

Invite the students to join hands in a circle. Make three large flash cards in red, yellow, and green. Instruct the students to walk quickly around the circle when you hold up the green card. Tell them to walk slowly when you hold up the yellow card, and to stop walking when you hold up the red card. Then hold the cards up in varying sequences.

Drama

Gather the students in a circle. Pick one student to be the traffic light. Have that student tell the other students to do something fast, slower, and then to stop.

Field Trip

Take the students for a walk to the nearest traffic light. Have the students watch the light turn red, yellow, and green. Point to the cars and ask the students to observe how they respond to the changing of the colors.

Jesse Owens

Jesse Cleveland Owens (1913-1980) was born in Oakville, Alabama. He became a famous American athlete by setting three track and field world records. Owens won four gold medals in the 1936 Olympic Games.

Jesse Owens could run, run, run!

People watched him in the sun, sun, sun!

He ran so fast, and he jumped so high.

If he only had wings, he could fly, fly, fly!

Rhyme
1. Which word rhymes with run? (sun)
2. Which word rhymes with high? (fly)
3. What other words rhyme with run? (fun, done, etc.)
4. What other words rhyme with high? (sky, try, etc.)

Comprehension
1. What is the name of this person? (Jesse Owens)
2. What did Jesse Owens do? (he ran and jumped)
3. How did he jump? (high)

Field Trip
Take the students to a local high school to see the track and field. Point out the hurdles and the lines on the track.

Gross Motor

Assemble four teams of four students each. Place one member of each team at each corner of the track. Give a baton to each student at the "starting corner" (which is also the finish line). Instruct the students with batons to race to the next corner and hand their batons to their team members, who will then do the same, till all runners have carried the baton and the final runners have crossed the finish line.

Place two pillows on the ground side by side. Let the students practice doing long jumps onto the pillows.

Math

Place four pillows on the ground, about two feet apart. Have the students count as they jump over each pillow.

Science

Tape a yardstick to a wall. Instruct the students to jump up as high as they can next to the yardstick. Measure each student's highest jump. Record and graph the results.

Leontyne Price

Leontyne Price was born in Laurel, Mississippi, in 1927. She was a great American soprano and performed with many opera companies, including the Metropolitan Opera. One of her famous roles was that of Bess in the opera "Porgy and Bess."

Leontyne *Price* could *sing* like a *bird.*

She *captured listeners* as she *sang* every *word.*

She *sang* in an *opera* called *"Porgy* and *Bess."*

Was it *beautiful? Yes, yes, yes!*

Rhyme
1. Which word rhymes with bird? (word)
2. Which word rhymes with Bess? (yes)
3. What other words rhyme with Bess? (mess, less, etc.)

Comprehension
1. What is the name of this person? (Leontyne Price)
2. What did she do? (sing)
3. Did she have a beautiful voice? (yes)
4. Do you think people liked to hear her sing? (any answer)

Circle
Ask each student to bring in a tape of some favorite music. Play some of the music during circle time for a musical version of "Show and Tell."

Drama

Ask each student to "sing like a bird." Obtain a tape recorder and record the students' singing. Play the tape and observe their reactions.

Art

Let the students make "record albums." Cut out large circles from tagboard. Give the students black paint and allow them to paint the circles black (or use black construction paper). Paste contrasting smaller circles onto the centers of the large circles. Write the names of songs and/or bands on the smaller circles. Make covers for the albums by taping slightly larger squares together on three sides. Let the students decorate their covers.

Science

Gather the students in a circle. Put a record player in the middle of the circle. Pass a record around and ask each student to describe it. Point out the tiny lines and tell them that this is where the music comes from. Play the record for the students. Let each student have an opportunity to put the needle on the record.

Jackie Robinson

John "Jackie" Robinson (1919-1972) was born in Cairo, Georgia. He became the first black baseball player to play in the American major leagues. Robinson joined the Dodgers in 1947 and was named Rookie of the Year. He received the Most Valuable Player award in 1947.

Jackie Robinson, what do you see?

I see a baseball looking at me.

Jackie, Jackie, whatcha gonna do?

I'm gonna knock that ball straight into the blue!

Jackie, Jackie, tell us who you are.

They call me Jackie Robinson, a baseball star!

Rhyme
1. Which word rhymes with see? (me)
2. Which word rhymes with do? (blue)
3. Which word rhymes with are? (star)
4. What other words rhyme with blue? (you, two, etc.)

Comprehension
1. What is the name of this person? (Jackie Robinson)
2. What did he do? (play baseball)
3. What did Robinson do to a baseball? (knocked it into the blue)
4. What is the "blue"? (the sky)

Math
Ask the students the following:
1. How many times do you hear the word *Jackie*? (six)

2. How many times do you hear the word *Robinson*? (two)
3. How many times do you hear the word *see*? (two)
4. How many times do you hear the word *me*? (two)

Game/Gross Motor

Let the students practice being baseball pitchers. Prepare a board with a big hole in the middle. Line up the students and give them three beanbags to pitch through the hole. Record their successes.

Gross Motor 2

Obtain several baseball mitts and balls. Take the class outdoors. Divide the class into two groups. Give mitts to the students in one group, and balls to those in the second group. Let the students toss the balls underhand to the students with the mitts several times, then switch groups.

Resource Person

Ask an adult associated with the sports world to come to the class to discuss the characteristics associated with good sportsmanship. Help the students develop a list of questions to ask the visitor.

Music

Practice singing "Take Me Out To The Ball Game."

Carl Rowan

Carl Thomas Rowan was born in Ravenscroft, Tennessee, in 1925. An American journalist, he was director of the U.S. Information Agency and was the first black American to serve on the National Security Council. Rowan was also an ambassador to Finland. He received national awards for his work in journalism.

RAP

Carl Rowan *talked* and he *wrote* about the *news.*

He *talked* and he *wrote* about the *good* and the *blues.*

He *talked* and he *wrote* about the *aged* and the *youth.*

He *talked* and he *wrote* because he *loved* the *truth.*

Rhyme
1. Which word rhymes with news? (blues)
2. Which word rhymes with youth? (truth)
3. What other words rhyme with youth? (tooth, booth, etc.)

Comprehension
1. What is the name of this person? (Carl Rowan)
2. What did he do? (he was a journalist, ambassador, etc.)
3. What did Rowan talk and write about? (news, good, blues, aged, youth)

Drama
Before your class begins Circle Time, give a microphone to one student. Let that student be the newscaster. He or she can ask members of the classroom where they would like to play (block area, house area, outdoors, etc.) and why.

Circle

Tape a portion of the local news and show it to your class. Record their observations.

Science

Obtain a camcorder that can film people live. Hook it up and let the students see themselves on television. If you don't have a live hook-up, tape a film of the students and play it back on the VCR.

Math

Let the students count the number of commercials they see or hear while listening to a television or radio news program.

Field Trip

Take the students to a local television or radio studio. Let them see how the cameras and lights work and how the news is brought to the "air."

Wilma Rudolph

Wilma Rudolph was born in St. Bethlehem, Tennessee, in 1940. Although she had polio as a youth, she grew up to become a great athlete. In 1960, Rudolph became the first American woman to win three gold medals in track and field at the Olympic Games. She set world records in the 100-meter and 200-meter races.

Wilma Rudolph was a *star, star, star!*
She *won* gold *medals* running *far, far, far!*
She *overcame sickness* with *courage* and *will.*
To *see* her *run* gave a *thrill, thrill, thrill!*

Rhyme
1. Which word rhymes with star? (far)
2. Which word rhymes with will? (thrill)
3. What other words rhyme with star? (car, bar, jar, etc.)
4. What other words rhyme with will? (spill, fill, till, etc.)

Comprehension
1. What is the name of this person? (Wilma Rudolph)
2. What did she do? (she ran)
3. How many gold medals did Rudolph win? (three)
4. What disease did she have? (polio)
5. Do you think she was a strong woman? (any answer)

Music
Sing "The Star Spangled Banner." Role-play an Olympic

awards ceremony during which an American athlete receives a gold medal.

Gross Motor

Let the students practice the long jump. Take them out to the sand area. Place a stick to indicate where the students should start their jump. Measure and record the lengths of their jumps.

Art

Let your students make gold medals.Cut circles out of tagboard and pass them out to the students. Give them yellow paint or crayons to decorate their medals. Punch two holes in the top of each medal and thread yarn through the holes so the students can wear their medals.

Science

Have a "Tennis Shoe Day." Ask everyone to wear tennis shoes. Gather the students in a circle and ask each student to describe characteristics of his or her tennis shoes.

Math

Bring plenty of sports magazines to class. Pass them out and give each student scissors. Instruct the students to cut out every tennis shoe they see. When everyone is finished, count the shoes.

Madame C. J. Walker

Madame C. J. Walker (1867-1919) was born Sarah Breedlove on a Louisiana cotton plantation. She invented haircare and cosmetic products that made her the wealthiest black woman in the United States. As she trained women to work as Walker agents, she taught them the value of independence and self-confidence.

Madame *Walker* made *people* look *neat, neat, neat!*
With *lipstick* and *cream,* it was a *treat, treat, treat!*
She made *hair* look *shiny* and *bright, bright, bright!*
She could *make* you *glisten* in the *light, light, light!*

Rhyme
1. Which word rhymes with neat? (treat)
2. Which word rhymes with bright? (light)
3. How many times do you hear the word *neat?* (three) *treat?* (three)

Comprehension
1. What is the name of this person? (Madame C. J. Walker)
2. What did she do for people? (any answer)
3. What could she do for hair? (make it look shiny and bright)
4. What is lipstick used for? (any answer)
5. What is cream used for? (any answer)

Drama
Obtain makeup, hats, and wigs. Pretend to be Madame

Walker and ask the students how they want to make themselves up. Students will have lots of fun getting themselves "fixed up."

Art

You will need blown-up balloons, yarn, paste, and assorted paints for this activity. Pass out the materials and instruct the students to pretend to be beauticians. Let the students paint faces on the balloons and use the yarn to make hair.

Science

Let the students make "Shampoo Bubble Makers." Give each student a foam cup and pipe cleaner. Help the students make small rings with the pipe cleaners for blowing bubbles. Fill the cups with a small amount of shampoo mixed with four tablespoons of water. Let the students blow bubbles.

Booker T. Washington

Booker Taliaferro Washington (1856-1915) was born a slave in Franklin County, Virginia. He became an educational leader of the black people in the United States. He established and headed the Tuskegee Institute in Alabama, wrote his autobiography *Up From Slavery*, and was elected to the American Hall of Fame.

Booker T. Washington was born to lead.

He *worked* very *hard* so he *would* succeed.

He *founded* a *school* (Tuskegee was its *name)*,

Wrote a *book,* and was elected to the *Hall* of *Fame.*

Rhyme
1. Which word rhymes with lead? (succeed)
2. Which word rhymes with name? (Fame)
3. What other words rhyme with lead? (seed, weed, etc.)

Comprehension
1. What is the name of this person? (Booker T. Washington)
2. What did he do? (any acceptable answer)
3. What was the name of the school he established? (Tuskegee)
4. What do you think people did at his school? (any answer)

Field Trip
If you are fortunate enough to have a museum that contains African art nearby, take the students to see it. Talk about the unique qualities of the art. Take pictures so the students can recall the visit.

Art

Give to each student a piece of 8½" x 11" white paper and some crayons. Tell each to draw a picture of what he or she wants to be. When the children have completed their drawings, find a photo of each child, glue it to his or her drawing, and roll up the drawing to make a scroll.

Drama

Give each student some building blocks. Let them pretend to be Booker T. Washington, building schools with their blocks. Record their observations.

Math

Ask the students to count the number of blocks they used to build their "schools." Make a graph of your findings.

Ethel Waters

Ethel Waters (1900-1977) was born in Chester, Pennsylvania. She became a famous American singer and actress, appearing on stage and in films. Among her most popular songs were "Dinah" and "Stormy Weather." Waters also wrote an autobiography, *His Eye Is on the Sparrow*.

Ethel Waters loved the *night*club *lights*.

She sang *soft* and *low* in the *cool*, dark *night*.

Not *only* could she *sing*, but she *acted* very *well*.

If you *saw* her in a *movie*, you'd be *caught* in her *spell*.

Rhyme
1. Which word rhymes with lights? (night)
2. Which word rhymes with well? (spell)
3. What are some other words that rhyme with light? (fight, right, sight, etc.)
4. What are some other words that rhyme with spell? (fell, tell, bell, etc.)

Comprehension
1. Who sang under nightclub lights? (Ethel Waters)
2. Did Ms. Waters sing loudly or softly? (softly)
3. What else could Ethel Waters do? (act)
4. Do you think that she could act well? (yes) Why? (any answer)

Drama

Let the students practice acting skills. Gather the students in a group. Pick one and whisper something you want him or her to act out. Ask the other students to try to guess what the student is acting out. For younger students you may wish to let the entire class to take part in the acting.

Drama 2

Obtain a puppet theatre and a female puppet or doll. Give each student an opportunity to use the puppet or doll to perform an Ethel Waters act or song on stage.

Science

Let the students make "movies." Give each student about six index cards. Let each student draw something related to a particular topic on each card. For example, if a child chooses to make an animal movie, let him or her draw animal pictures on the cards to create a story. Staple the tops of the cards together, bend, and let go! The student will see things move.

Science 2

To show students the simple mechanics of movies, bring in a slide projector and slides. Let the students look at the slides and put them into the projector. Show them how the light makes the picture show up on the screen.

Daniel Hale Williams

Daniel Hale Williams (1856-1931) was born in Hollidaysburg, Pennsylvania. He became a doctor in Chicago and was later appointed director of Freeman's Hospital in Washington, D.C. Williams was the only black charter member of the American College of Surgeons, which was founded in 1913. In 1893, he performed the first successful surgical closure of a wound to the heart.

Daniel Williams was a *surgeon*, good with *knives*.

He *made* it his *business* to *heal* and to save *lives*.

He *was* a good *doctor*, he was *skillful* and *smart*.

He *helped* many *people* with dis*ease*s of the *heart*.

Rhyme
1. Which word rhymes with knives? (lives)
2. Which word rhymes with smart? (heart)
3. What other words rhyme with smart? (cart, tart, part, etc.)

Comprehension
1. What is the name of this person? (Daniel Hale Williams)
2. What did he do? (he was a doctor)
3. What are some of the things that doctors do? (any answer)
4. Can you point to where your heart is? (middle of chest)

Field Trip
If possible, arrange to visit a local hospital or doctor's office. If this is not possible, invite a doctor or nurse to visit the

classroom to discuss their role as a professional health care worker. Help the students prepare a list of questions to ask the visitor.

Science

Obtain a stethoscope from a drugstore or a hospital. Let the students listen to their hearts. Record their observations.

Art

Discuss with students exercises that are good for the heart. Provide drawing paper and crayons and ask each student to draw a picture of him- or herself engaged in an activity that is good for the heart.

Health

Discuss the importance of a good diet to developing and maintaining a healthy heart. List "harmful foods for the heart" and "healthful foods for the heart" in two separate columns on the board. Ask students to evaluate their own eating habits in terms of the two lists.

Food

Plan and prepare a school snack or a special picnic lunch made up of only "heart healthy" foods.